PRABODH SIRUR

IN THE
WONDERLAND
OF TALENT MANAGEMENT

a corporate fairy tale

ISBN: 1-4392-4462-6

ISBN-13: 9781439244623

Library of Congress Control Number: 2009905521

Visit www.booksurge.com to order additional copies.

Here is what some of my friends, colleagues, and family members say about my effort.

"*In the Wonderland of Talent Management* is one of those rare books with real power in its simplicity.

"It raises our horizons beyond the daily grind and challenges us intellectually, emotionally and spiritually.

"With a sense of drama and humor, Prabodh takes us on a journey with a truly inspired CEO who can see to the heart of his organization and revitalize it.

"The book's enthusiasm and passion are infectious. It even ends on a practical note, gently taking us back to our daily world, but with ideas for transforming it. Buy it, read it (it won't take you long), and then renew yourself and your organization!"

—*Michael Gates, Finland*

"A concept like 'Atlantis' could bring (back) a lot of company pride, work satisfaction, enthusiasm, etc., to all our people.

- The principle of "Docendo Discimus" is something which works so well.

- The story of the Bodhi tree is a great one; so simple yet effective.

- About one and a half years ago all Dutch managers had a session where they had to paint our corporate values. The paintings are still hanging in the reception in the building in Amstelveen."

—*Jan Willem van Doorn, the Netherlands*

"I enjoyed reading your first book and thanks for choosing me to review it, quite an honor.

"At the end of the day if anyone is really passionate about something, they will put their heart, soul and time into it and it is this type of enthusiasm that we need to get into our companies to help to make the difference between an ok and a really innovative and growing company."

—Gillian Hardy, UK

"After reading the book I was feeling so elated that I could not resist thanking you for writing such a nice book which will surely improve work environment of many organizations.

"When I was reading the book I was imagining myself as 'PN' (as we do while watching a movie, we imagine ourselves as the hero) and after the success of each project I was feeling as if it was I who had succeeded."

—Ashutosh Tripathy, India

"This is a great thought stimulator. We need to think outside the box so much more than we do, and these stories help us to see possibilities."

—Justin Hooper, UK

"If one ventured to look for a Primer to *Fountainhead*, I JUST FOUND IT!! A must-read for every manager worth his salt."

—Srikar Baljekar, India

"Frankly it is one of most inspiring books I have read so far.

"The scope of the book is not limited to a large company or HR people. The scope is far beyond this.

"Every person who wants to take initiative in his/her organization must read this book."

—*Asim Chowdhury, India*

"Your book isn't very fairy tale in the wonderland...Your book will help bring out the core passion of every individual/institution for the benefit of self and the surroundings someday."

—*Veronica Ezekiel, India*

"The idea of managing and retaining talents by encouraging and supporting employees' passions is extraordinary.

"The book goes one step further and shows innovative ways of implementing this idea. This book will definitely inspire today's PNs to become John Galt.

"This book truly reflects your passion of motivating people. I really acknowledge you for highlighting this area of human resources which normally goes unnoticed."

—*Kunal Padia, India*

"*Atlas Shrugged* is one amongst the many books that I have enjoyed. Another book that I appreciated and still remember is *Animal Farm* by George Orwell. This book by Prabodh is similar in the sense that it leaves a lasting impact. What I received from the book is much more than what I had expected (why hadn't I expected too much?—because I thought I had already read a lot and there was not much that could surprise me in the field of people retention and motivation. It shows that we should always be humble)."

—*Mithilesh Kumar, India*

This book is dedicated to the CEOs of the world who make their employees feel special.

CONTENTS

FOREWORD

Docendo discimus is Latin for "by teaching, we learn"—a motto for several famous educational institutions around the globe. Prabodh Sirur has used the concept very innovatively to explain an "engaged organization."

PN, the CEO, works with several team members to create an environment in which engagement is by choice and has generated enthusiasm to create a new "Atlantis." While every organization has its unique programs and initiatives to remain an employer of choice, the thought and the process to create Atlantis is indeed unique.

I have personally experienced that such engagements do bond the team far more effectively than traditional methods. Once our team got together to support a local community. At the same time we created long-lasting bonds within ourselves and were driven toward another important social objective, aside from what each one did in the office.

When I read "by teaching, we learn," I paused for a couple of minutes. How true! Prabodh Sirur has re-reminded us about the term to explain how it can be a powerful tool to engage employees in productive and collaborative initiatives to support the organization as well as the larger society.

As with every organization, managing a collection of intelligent people is a challenging job for the CEO—retaining them as well as channeling their talent productively. Prabodh has beautifully interwoven the theory of multiple intelligences to demonstrate the power of collective intellect.

Anyone can lead a group at the foothills, but to get to the top, one needs the excellent teamwork, innovation, and collaboration that only true leaders can inspire. This story is about leadership through employee engagement and collective intelligence.

Success is built by the expertise of employees who use circumstances as opportunities to develop innovative solutions. The example of teaching yoga to employees of clients explains the concept of value beyond contract and its impact on clients.

Each situation in an organization needs different talent to achieve the desired results and, hence, proper harvesting of different talents. The rainbow of employee talents is key to success for every leader. PN demonstrates through each example that creation of a forum for employees to express themselves takes them on a successful journey of which they never dreamt.

The book should be a must read, not just for the leaders but for everyone; it will inspire them to think of innovative solutions and create an Atlantis.

—Abhay Gupte, CEO, Logica India

INTRODUCTION

Talent management is associated with the phrases *employee attraction, employee growth,* and *employee retention.*

The focus is on how much the employee can give rather than "what is possible" for the employee to give.

The employees' focus is wholly on how they can improve the talents required for the job.

They have neither the time nor the resources to bring to the table the talent that nature gave them. I found very few who said, "These are my key faculties, and I am actually using them daily in my work life."

There always will be a few hundred jobs chased by a few thousand; people are therefore forced to showcase only those skills that are required for the job and not their real talents.

At the end of their careers, many people are a little empty because they could not put their core talents to use in their work life.

This book attempts to address this problem. It provides a framework for an organization to realize the untapped potential of its employees. It provides a few ways to make employees feel special.

The book contains fairytales to give readers a preview of what is possible in a corporate world when CEOs make it their role to unleash the dreams, talents, and passions of their people.

Although the backdrop used for this book is a large IT company in India, the premise is relevant to all organizations.

The inspirers who supplied me with the thought material to build this book are Howard Gardner and Ayn Rand.

Howard Gardner's theory on *multiple intelligences* (1983) revolutionized the field of education. If his thinking can change the way the schools are run, it can do the same for the corporate world too.

Ayn Rand's book *Atlas Shrugged* (1957) took the world by storm with its inspirational thought about the human spirit. *Atlas Shrugged* is about John Galt, a metaphorical Atlas of Greek mythology, who creates a secret city, *Atlantis*, to charm away the geniuses of the world.

My book implores people to create an *Atlantis* within. With each act covered in this book, PN (the hero of this book) pleases John Galt!

You will observe that many stories have a similar beginning and a similar end; the repetition is by design, to emphasize the point—the employees have their talents exploited for their own wellbeing!

All the stories are around PN, the CEO. You may wonder if he does any other work. This is again by design; I want to emphasize the point that some of the ideas covered in the book are indeed possible, only when the CEO makes up his or her mind to make them happen.

The book mentions some people and institutions that exist in the real world. Their deeds inspired me to include them and weave stories around them. I recognize them below:

Sanjeev Kapoor is a well-known chef and author of books on Indian cuisine. He also enjoys celebrity status because of his TV appearances. He is the recipient of many awards, including the Best Cookery Show Award by the Indian Television Academy. Sanjeev participates in prestigious world conferences as a speaker or a culinary panel member. (http://www.sanjeevkapoor.com)

Michael van Gessel is a famous landscape designer from the Netherlands. He has received top international awards in landscape design and is also an author of books on landscape designing. (www.michaelvangessel.com)

M. F. Husain is known as the "Picasso of India" and is one of the country's best-known artists. He is the highest paid painter in India. A single canvas fetched him about $2 million at Christie's. He has also produced and directed a few movies. (http://www.mfhussain.com)

Vigyan Ashram is an institute that imparts technical and entrepreneurial training to rural school dropouts. Srinath Kalbag, Scientist Emeritus, at Levers and his wife Meera Kalbag created the institute. The successful education program they created is a subject of academic study and a replicable model. (http://www.vigyanashram.com)

The Key Learning Community in Indianapolis, is probably the first Multiple Intelligences School to be based on Howard Gardner's theory. (http://www.616.ips.k12.in.us)

The Inter-University Centre for Astronomy and Astrophysics, Pune, India, is a center of excellence for teaching, research, and development in astronomy and astrophysics. (http://www.iucaa.ernet.in/Home.html)

Prabodh Sirur

Bangalore

PN, CEO
— CREATING ATLANTIS

This is the story of PN, CEO of a large information technology company, who believed that his real role was to create a new world for his people.

It all began on Sept 8 2006. PN was going through the monthly management report. He suddenly stopped reading when he came across the employee turnover part of the report.

He was concerned that his employees were going away to work for someone else.

Some of those who had been part of the team that created a brand worth a billion dollars for his company were no longer with him. The employee turnover costs for the past twelve months were a staggering three hundred million US dollars.

PN thought the people working for him were proud to be part of their organization. Then why was this happening?

PN went through the statistics once more. Most of his employees were between the ages of twenty and thirty; they were bright young minds with great enthusiasm. Maybe his organization did not give them a field in which to blossom fully.

In the beginning, PN felt that his job was to help people find meaning in their work, create a culture where more and more people would want to join him, create a dreamland for everyone, a place where one could realize one's dream, a place where one could dream larger than life.

But what were people doing in his company now? Weren't they more like robots, churning out productivity figures, input-process-output, input-process-output?

When they had joined his organization, they had been full of aspirations about their lives. What had happened to their passions? What had happened to the dreams they buried for the needs of the organization?

He was not happy with the supposedly innovative solutions given by his advisors for "managing attrition." Their suggestions included:

- give productivity bonuses;

- give spot awards;

- plan job rotation;

- give them flexible work hours or allow them to work from home;

- initiate team building, or sports activities;

- invite family members for company functions;

- pay for a day of golf;

- introduce work-life balance, build child care centers, start counseling services, or concierge services.

Now it all looked cheap; he felt he was, by doing all this, actually insulting the real owners of the wealth, the owners of a magnificent organization created by the employees.

His role was much more than "managing attrition." It was to create an environment in which people achieved something about which they cared passionately. And it was to generate possibilities for his people, to bring out the passions they had buried deep down, to rekindle their core interests.

He felt like John Galt—the same John Galt who created an Atlantis.

Read on, to know what PN did to reap a fortune
from the untapped talents in his people. Read on, if you
want to create an Atlantis in your organization.

∽

DOCENDO DISCIMUS

(pronounced as: dȯ-ˌken-dō-ˈdis-ki-ˌmu̇s)

June 15, 2010: PN was looking with a sense of satisfaction at the three envelopes spread on his table. He felt he had more than repaid his debt to the teachers from his village school. The three envelopes carried letters of a very unusual nature. No IT CEO would have received such letters in the past.

The letters were from the governors of three different states, inviting him to receive the Best Teacher Award, on behalf of his company, on Teachers' Day. It was really a record of sorts; a company, rather than an individual, had been nominated as best teacher.

PN's mind went back three years. That was when this new revolution had started in his organization. It was on June 2, 2007, when he invited all his team members for an off-site meeting with a single agenda—unusual corporate social responsibility (CSR).

When the team met, each member was excited and knew PN would come up with something very unusual. They also knew there was going to be an additional work put on them, but they were more than willing. The organization was respected as "thought leaders," and they were all proud about it.

PN started with the customary words about where the organization was and where it was headed.

When the curiosity about the day's agenda reached a peak, PN paused and then flashed the statement on the screen—*Docendo Discimus*.

The people in the room could have had huge question marks over their heads the way their faces looked. They all waited eagerly for PN's explanation. He turned to them and started explaining.

"Friends, we are known for the quality of our delivery. We have maintained our employer-of-the-year status for the past three years. Our names appear in the agenda of our competitors as a threat. Our widening global presence is recognized all over, and we are on the top-five employer lists of most colleges."

Everyone waited, still wondering what this docendo discimus meant. PN continued.

"Times are changing. We are finding it difficult to keep better-quality people working in the company. If we do not act now, it will be difficult for us to meet our target of becoming a company of one-hundred and twenty-thousand people by 2010.

"Our campus recruitment team is doing a great job. A fifth of our new entrants are new graduates. But there are murmurs about the quality of these people, the quality of teaching in their colleges, and the outdated curriculum, which doesn't match the needs of today's industry.

"Our board is not happy about the huge cost we have to invest in the additional training to the *freshers* who take six months to be ready to work on client projects. We need to reduce these timelines; we need to have better people on projects faster."

Mohan, head of human resources, pricked up his ears. But these costs were well-justified. After all, every large company faced the same problems waiting for new recruits to achieve corporate standards. He was well aware of the quality of education and was already in discussion with colleges all over on how to improve the curriculum.

Suresh, the finance guy, was aware of the talks in the last board meeting about the rising cost on people and the impact it had on the margins. There was going to be no additional money, should PN come up with something new. Yet at the end of this meeting, he sensed that he was going to have to scoop out some money and build a solid justification for the board for whatever PN would propose.

PN continued, waving his hand towards the screen.

"Docendo discimus is a Latin term that means, 'we learn when we teach.' People add to themselves when they give knowledge to someone. This also means that we send our employees out to teach and, in turn, grow them into better people."

Everyone gaped at PN. This made no sense to them.

"PN," said Anand, the delivery strategist, "we are in the business of delivering software solutions, not teaching. The world around us is outsourcing its non-core business, and you are asking us to take on some business that has nothing to do with us."

PN smiled and said, "Yes, I am asking the organization to do this. When I explain the full scenario, you will agree with me." He continued.

"The solution I am proposing will have manifold benefits. It will have a better hit rate in our campus recruitment; it will reduce our fresher training duration. Not only that, this will improve our brand recall, it will improve our employee satisfaction and retention, and it will improve our margins."

Everyone in the room became a little restless. They were clueless as to how on earth all this could improve the brand equity, the CSR, and above all, the margins.

PN went to the next slide on the screen: Prepare our key employees from all levels to go out and ask them to teach in colleges.

There were questions in some people's minds. How would the education department allow this? The key employees were already burdened. How will they find time to prepare *and* teach?

But a few saw some meaning in what PN was saying. Suchitra, head of resourcing, said, "PN, you know what some of our old timers keep saying? They tell me that when they retire, they would like to go back to the universities and teach. Only then will they feel they have served the community."

"Spot on, Suchitra. And look at what will happen when we give this opportunity to them now, well in advance of their retirement. They will be tremendously happy about this.

"Folks, people won't mind doing all this, even giving their personal time. Especially if we recognize their efforts and reward them.

"What I propose is:

- we get our experienced employees together and agree on what we want to teach;

- we give them world-class training from a world-class institute on how to train and how to teach;

- we ask them to choose the colleges and the topics and to take a teaching session once a year.

"I am sure that many who come forward to take this up will actually choose their hometowns as places to teach and feel happy that they have.

"I am aware there are doubts in our minds on how to sell this to our people, the educational institutions, our shareholders, and the board. But I also know that you collectively will come up with solutions to address all this.

"Take the rest of the day to work on this. Together you have always come up with something really smart, and I know this time will be no exception.

"So, by the end of the day I would like to hear your ideas on first, how to sell this to our employees, meet their aspirations, and reward and recognize them; second, how to sell this to our shareholders, to the media, improve brand recall, sell CSR, and improve margins; and third, how to sell this to the educational institutions."

The team members put their heads together for the rest of the afternoon and, as usual, came back with something stunning. The idea that had seemed so farfetched in the morning looked most convincing, once they had all debated, discussed and distilled their thoughts into actions.

Their key ideas were:

- enhance employees' satisfaction by offering them an opportunity to grow outside their work, to address their social aspirations, and to receive world-class training to equip them to teach effectively;

- recognize their efforts by including this contribution in the employees' database and embossing one star for each year of teaching onto their photo id cards;

- record input from students who had benefited from the teaching, from employees who went out and taught;

- create stories for all the PR campaigns and include a mention in the annual reports.

The best idea that came from the business group was what they called "cub sourcing" which meant that the organization should not stop after teaching the students. It should create a mechanism by which various pieces of work could be outsourced to students, the cubs.

This idea of cub sourcing was picked up for debate and improvement. Everyone felt the idea had fantastic potential. It provided an opportunity for students to do "real work." It allowed for the organization to assess people's caliber and identify future employees, and it provided the opportunity for the businesses to actually get work done at lower cost. The work could be as complex as writing software components, test cases, or simple documentation.

At the end of the deliberations, everyone looked very excited about what they had created. They could actually sense the excitement that docendo discimus was going to create in the market, a new topic being debated among the management gurus.

PN looked at his team with pride and told them, "Great work, as usual, guys. I can clearly envision the results of what you came up with today. I see about five thousand people, trained by our people, on board in the next three years, productive almost on day one. I see about one percent of our people, our future leaders, showing off their docendo discimus stars on their badges. I see a hundred colleges spread across the country covered under this program. And I see revenue coming from cub sourcing having a direct positive impact on our bottom line.

"Congratulations. You've done a great service to the organization, to our people, to the student community, and to our customers."

The dream he sold to his lieutenants three years ago had actually became a reality. His employees loved being part of this revolution. The students loved it. The media splashed rave stories about the organization's contributions to society. Colleges were proud to display a sign that read: "Our students are taught by the stars from the best employer of the year." The management gurus loved the term *cub sourcing* and started building case studies around it.

PN came back to the present. His eyes rested on the three invitation letters on the table. The result of the hard work of all his people was in front of him: public recognition of his organization—the Best Teacher Award for 2010 from three states.

ᑭᗢ

Bodhi Shopping

June 2, 2011: PN had a smile on his face when he looked at the news headline: "Millionth Bodhi tree exported."

No one would have believed that a small beginning in his organization four years ago could have developed into such a strange business proposition for his country.

It was some time in April 2007 when his team met to discuss the itinerary of the Japanese prime minister's visit to his organization.

Details of the agenda were finalized, details of the prime minister's tour of the facility were drawn, and the guest list was finalized.

The agenda was to include a gift for the visitor. Various suggestions included a gem-studded statue of Buddha.

Gagan, the head of business development and also an environmental champion in the organization, made an unusual suggestion. "Why don't we present him with a Bodhi tree?"

The team members looked at him as if they did not understand the simple question. It was indeed a strange suggestion.

Every Indian knew what the Bodhi tree was. It was the tree under which Buddha, the originator of Buddhism, received enlightenment two-thousand five-hundred years ago. The tree was a place of pilgrimage and was visited by tens of thousands of people annually from all over the world.

How could someone suggest such a strange gift?

Gagan sat up straight to explain. "Well, it was just a thought. It just flashed in my mind when you mentioned the gem-studded Buddha. You are aware that today we can create clones. I am sure it will not be difficult to create a clone from the Bodhi tree."

There was silence in the room. People just did not know what to say.

PN broke the silence. "Well, Gagan, this seems a very wild thought, but I guess if we can make this happen, the Japanese prime minister will feel honored. It will be a pleasant surprise for him and also for his countrymen. One thing I am sure of, they will never forget our name. Can you look into this and let us know?"

"But what about the costs?" asked Suvarna, the CFO. "How much is it going to be and which cost center are we attributing this to?"

Anand, the delivery strategist, who had seen the world, said, "PN, I must remind you that this is not our business. We are a systems integration company and have nothing to do with this area."

"Anand, Suvarna, I agree with you on this," PN said. "Gagan, can you get some more information on the costs? Maybe the management team can afford this and give it as a personal gift from all of us, rather than from the organization. I do not want to let go of this thought, though it looks too good to be true."

AVL, the quality assurance head, said, "I agree that it is possible to create clones, but who will allow us to touch the tree?"

The team did not speak about the topic much after this because they thought this was just a fantasy idea that would be forgotten as the days passed. They discussed other aspects of the prime minister's visit and then the meeting broke off.

After the meeting, Gagan caught hold of Abid, the administration head, who was a well-connected person and could be of help. They met the head of the botanical department.

They got to know more about something called somatic embryogenesis and about micro propagation. They sought contacts of the Micropropagation Technology Park, Pune, where a lot of work in the area of tissue culture was happening.

They also learned that they were not the first ones to clone the Bodhi tree. It had first been done by Sanghamitra, daughter of King Ashoka, way back in 288 B.C., when she carried a sapling of the original tree to Anuradhapura, Sri Lanka, and that this was the oldest living human-planted tree.

They also learned that Dr. Narlikar, a scientist and head of Inter-University Centre for Astronomy and Astrophysics in Pune, had done a similar experiment. Dr. Narlikar's team successfully grew the clone of the famous apple tree under which Isaac Newton had sat and is said to have thought of the theory of gravity. Gagan was elated to know that what he proposed was actually possible.

Gagan asked for PN's help to meet with the Ministry of Science and Technology. Gagan prepared a proposal in which PN's organization would fund the initial efforts.

They also negotiated for their organization's name to be tagged to the project.

They told the minister about the great potential of selling millions of plants from the Bodhi tree to Far East countries that hold the tree in the high esteem.

The minister agreed to look into it. Later, they were informed that the work could to be undertaken under the aegis of Dr. Tendurkar of Micropropagation Technology Park in Pune.

This was great news. Gagan assembled his team of environmental enthusiasts and went to meet Dr. Tendurkar. The group gained great insight into the science of tissue culture. Some of Gagan's team members stayed back to work with Dr. Tendurkar.

The pilot project, of which many were dying to be part, gave the team a great sense of satisfaction. Each day was a one to be remembered forever. The news about this gift was kept within the team.

The grand day of the prime minister's visit arrived. There were the regular agenda items, during which the business groups presented him with the details of the contributions they had made to the Japanese economy, how their people had built smart systems that helped better governance, and so forth.

Then they took him on the facilities tour to show the environment they had created for their employees. The prime minister was happy. In the evening, they had a session with key employees at which the prime minister spoke highly of their organization and thanked the people for their contribution to his country.

At the end of the session, PN rose to give a word of thanks. He spoke of their long-term commitment to Japan, and he spoke about what his people had learned from the Japanese during their projects there. He concluded his speech by saying, "Your Excellency, Mr. Prime Minister, we would like to give you a small token of our respect. We are sure you will value our gesture." And he presented the small Bodhi sapling.

PN continued. "Your Excellency, this is a gift from us to your countrymen who are devotees of Gautam Buddha. It is a clone of the Bodhi tree, the tree under which Gautam Buddha attained enlightenment."

The prime minister was extremely touched by the gift. He took the small plant in his hands and bowed with reverence.

And this was the beginning of Project Bodhi, kicked off by the Micropropagation Technology Park. More and more plantlets were created in the nursery, and countries in the Far East lapped more of them up. Everyone wanted to have a Bodhi in his or her home.

The period the team spent in developing the Bodhi saplings in Micropropagation Technology Park was the greatest reward for them. They were passionate about the flora and fauna, and they were passionate about learning something new in this area. What better reward could they have received from their organization!

PN was deeply satisfied that he could provide a platform for his people to express themselves and be happy. It was a small victory for John Galt!

Did his people stop after this achievement? Of course not. They created Indian herbal gardens in the city, they generated interest in all employees to invest in a huge farm to start organic farming, and they created resorts on the farm for their parents to visit. They created small patches of land where their children could experiment and see nature's wonders, they helped the surrounding villagers set up self-help groups to work on their farms, and to learn and implement new technologies. The list is endless. But suffice it to say that a large number of employees of PN's company now had a forum within which to express themselves and that allowed them to embark on the kind of journey that previously might have only been a dream!

VALUFACTURE

December 12, 2007: PN received mail from Gyan, one of his project managers. Gyan's mail said, "PN, I am coming back from the project after two years in Delaware. I have something interesting to share."

An excited Gyan met PN and spoke about his experience on the project.

"PN, when I went there, I wondered how on earth I would spend my time after office hours. But as it turned out, I did meet some very interesting client employees. We would talk all about India—the snake charmers, and the elephants, and so on. They had all the usual questions. Many had the perception that snakes roam around everywhere in India, and that the place is full of elephants.

"During one of these discussions, I told them about yoga and that I am a certified yoga teacher. They asked me whether I could teach them yoga, and I was happy to do it. They did not have any yoga teachers around, and this was an opportunity for me to serve them.

"They took me to their HR people, and I gave them a presentation on yoga and its benefits to physical and mental health, showing how it helps improve relationships and productivity, and so on. I also told them that it had nothing to do with any religion; it was just a spiritual journey for a sound mind.

"They were happy with what they heard and asked me if I could teach yoga to any interested employees. They asked me how much I wanted to be paid for my time teaching. I told them this was my gift to our esteemed clients. Anyway, there was great enthusiasm and participation in the yoga sessions."

He showed PN the testimonials from the company and individuals.

"The best part was that the employees and the head of HR fought for my extension so that I could be around longer. This was the best experience of my life. Not only did I get more business for the company, but I also have the personal satisfaction of knowing that I can use my passion to help someone else. I wouldn't be surprised if the clients give us more projects, only because what we gave them was over and above their expectations of the contract."

PN thanked Gyan for sharing this with him. He arranged Gyan's meeting with Shoma, the company's PR person, and asked Gyan to repeat the story to Shoma so she could include it in the house magazine.

PN remembered Edward De Bono, the champion of lateral thinking, who spoke about "valufacture." He felt that what Gyan had created was an extra value to the project. What he had done had not been a contractual obligation but an unexpected offering to clients.

PN shared the Gyan story with his team members. They were proud. But they felt that this story was a success because Gyan had managed it in a mature manner. To make this a proposition that could be repeated, they wanted something formal to be drawn up.

Someone said, "PN, as you are aware, many of our people would give their right arms to stay on-site if they had to. If we tell them that one way to achieve this is to teach our clients what they themselves are good at, we could risk landing ourselves in all sorts of trouble."

There was consensus that there must be a proper mechanism to handle this. PN agreed and asked them to come up with some solutions.

Some time later, the team members met to discuss this. The conversation was dynamic and spirited.

"Do we know how many people know yoga in our organization? And how many are certified?"

"There are many branches of yoga; which one do you want to teach?"

"Guys, I think we should leave how to deal with the client to the individual project manager."

"Why do you want to stick to yoga alone? There are many things our people can teach."

"Like what? Riding elephants? Snake charming?"

"Oh, come on. You know Indian cooking is all the rage. They could teach them cooking."

"Forget it. I've seen westerners cooking better Indian food than any one of us in this room. Everything is available on the Internet, and everyone sells ready-to-cook Indian meals."

"We don't have information on our people's capabilities; we don't know whether our offering is going to be of value to clients, and we don't know what kind of legal hassles we could land ourselves in. On top of all that, we are saying that this is a free service. I have never seen a better business proposition!"

"Great, you know, you actually stated all the pain statements. If we work on each of them, we'll find a solution."

"Fantastic! I agree with you that valufacture does not mean we should give it for free. But when we want to exchange something for money, it should be contractual."

"So the question is, how do we contract? Are we going to say in the contract, 'along with the software, we will also provide 250 man hours of yoga to the client organization?' That looks a little silly. I hope the clients don't cancel the whole contract because of it."

"I think, at this moment the best we can do is to get together the senior people, the project managers, and tell them about the Gyan story and leave it at that."

"Better still, we'll ask Gyan to tell the story. He'll feel happy sharing his experience. People can ask questions and get answers from the horse's mouth."

When the team next met PN, they told him what they thought—that the organization was not yet ready to institutionalize the Gyan experience. PN respected the team's view. Everyone agreed that after a formal recognition of Gyan's contribution at a meeting of senior managers the chapter would remain closed.

It was a very good meeting, and the managers asked Gyan useful questions. The meeting ended with everyone going away with different thoughts about Gyan's experience. Some of them repeated the story to their juniors; some of the juniors repeated the Gyan story to their juniors. But nothing happened on the matter of valufacture.

After some days, there was repeat business from the Delaware clients, who requested Gyan for the project. Gyan joined the project, and he knew many of his old friends were waiting for him and for their yoga meetings.

John Galt shrugged! He was patient. He was prepared to wait.

∽

DIY RESTAURANT

October 16, 2010: PN was looking at an advertisement in the newspaper. It was about the opening of a new kind of restaurant, called Do-It-Yourself Restaurant. It was a special restaurant for PN because it was owned and run by his employees.

It was a state-of-the-art restaurant, and its distinction was that you could go there with friends and cook a meal under the guidance of the restaurant's employees. Each cooking table was fitted with a video screen at which the celebrity chef Sanjeev Kapoor, the most celebrated face of Indian cuisine, instructed you on each and every step of the cooking.

PN's mind rewound three years. That was when this new revolution had started in his organization.

It was October 23, 2007. PN was flying from Mumbai to Bangalore, back to his office. He vaguely recalled that the person sitting to his left was some celebrity. *Ah yes*. He was Sanjeev Kapoor, the celebrity chef who had become an icon. PN congratulated Sanjeev on his achievements and wished him well. They had a good chat about what PN should eat at his age.

PN suddenly remembered that his organization was hosting a big corporate potluck lunch the next day. It was a great opportunity to invite Sanjeev, and he readily agreed to be there the next day. The potluck lunch was a great success. Everyone had brought something for his or her team. Some people had decorated their lunch tables using vegetables and fruits. It was a fun-filled atmosphere, and Sanjeev's presence added to the excitement.

Sanjeev appreciated the employee's efforts. He said, "It's no surprise that you engineers cook so well. I always consider cooking as a science and the kitchen as a laboratory."

PN thanked the celebrity chef for giving his time. Sanjeev, looking at the excited faces, said, "I enjoyed it too, and had I known about it earlier, I would have participated!"

PN could not resist an opportunity. "Well Sanjeev," he responded, "I will find a way for our people to see you more closely."

Soon after Sanjeev left, PN had a meeting with the team leaders of the potluck lunch. He congratulated them for the excitement it had created and the togetherness he sensed in the teams. He told them what he had promised Sanjeev Kapoor and asked them to come up with ideas on how to make it happen.

A large number of PN's young engineers worked on-site, with many relocating from far-away places, away from their families. Learning to cook, therefore, was a basic survival skill for them. PN wanted to focus on this need, with Sanjeev Kapoor's help.

Some days later, the team met with PN. They had come up with something very novel.

"We don't think we need Sanjeev Kapoor to teach us cooking, because every recipe is available on the Internet. But what we want to do is set up a restaurant, in partnership with him. A do-it-yourself restaurant."

PN was amused and curious. The team had a full-blown plan, including the funding side of it. They were quite excited at the prospect of discussing it.

"We'll run regular classes ourselves on weekends for our people to learn cooking. For many of us, cooking is a passion and so we don't mind spending time teaching our colleagues. But what we really want to do is set up a restaurant."

"But what do you know about running a restaurant?" PN asked.

"That's where we will need Sanjeev Kapoor's help. His association will bring about lot of publicity and credibility and professional help."

PN liked what he was hearing.

"We will do our own funding," a team member continued. "There are so many thousands of us in the company. People will definitely want to invest in this novel venture."

PN did not want to dampen their spirits. But he knew the excitement would pass once they got busy with their work. The only help they demanded from PN was the support from the company's commercial department, so that all the legalities would be taken care of.

PN said, "Well, ask them. If you 'sell' well, they will help you on their personal time, I am sure. I do not want this venture to be part of our main business. But count me in as far as personal investment is concerned."

The team went back full of anticipation. They met with Sanjeev Kapoor and told him the idea. Sanjeev was happy to be part of it. This was a one-of-a-kind restaurant, and he knew it made a lot of business sense in a city like Bangalore, where the young crowd would love to experiment with cooking.

The teams started their internal publicity and gathered many people to learn cooking. They started discussing the DIY restaurant. There was a good response to an idea that all employees could invest in the venture.

They started producing the instruction videos for several types of combinations of meals. The videos included music and jokes to make cooking interesting. It was a huge task, but then so many people were involved, all loved what they were doing.

There was a huge response when the "cooks" invited all the employees to invest. Sanjeev Kapoor invested his own stake in it. The "cooking stations" looked sleek, each with a screen and camera that allowed the guests to capture their cooking on video.

The restaurant site was completed. The look and feel and the publicity campaign were finalized, and employees were recruited. The stage was set for a grand opening.

It was one of the happiest moments for PN when the restaurant opened. He met the excited members at the restaurant. The dream his people sold him three years before had actually become a reality. His employees loved being part of this revolution. There was great excitement about the stamp they were going to put on their city.

The media splashed rave stories about the initiative of the employees' in PN's organization. Management experts sang the praises of the various ways the employees could be engaged for better employee satisfaction.

PN felt a deep sense of satisfaction for providing a platform on which his people could express themselves and be happy. It was yet another victory for John Galt!

Did his people stop after this achievement? Of course not. They taught Indian cuisine to their clients' employees, they taught hygiene and cooking to a lot of women from villages, and they created careers for them (the dial-a-cook project). Their three-course meal videos became famous. The list is endless.

Suffice it to say that a large number of employees of PN's company now had a forum in which to express themselves and embark on the kind of journey that would previously only have been a dream!

∽

PLUCK THE FLOWERS
AND LEAVES

June 2, 2009: PN was looking at a letter from his key client. It was a request for help to create an Indian herbal garden in their office.

PN recalled the client's visit when their team was taken for a tour of the Indian herbal garden created by his employees. They were impressed by the concept and even more so by the signs around the garden: "Please pluck the flowers and leaves." It was not the usual, "Do Not Touch" sign one always saw in parks.

The garden consisted of a large number of Indian herbs and medicinal plants. Under each plant there was information on its medicinal properties, the names of the diseases that could be cured, the "leafage" (dosage) for each disease, and so on. The "gardeners" encouraged people to pluck the leaves and eat them.

This garden was the work of enthusiastic employees from the world environment group. They were passionate about the medicinal plants. They had done extensive research on each of the plants and collected useful information for the visitors.

The client wanted a similar garden on their campus. The request was just unbelievable, especially because the client was from the Netherlands, a country famous for flowers and gardens. The renowned Michael van Gessel had done their existing thematic landscaping. PN only hoped it was not a joke!

He recalled how it had all started. The company's world environment group had wanted something more to do. A few of its members were already working on some secret tissue culture project, but the remaining members were looking for a new project.

Someone from the group found out about the herbal garden in Rashtrapati Bhavan, the residence of the President of India and discovered that the National Botanical Research Institute (NBRI) had designed it. They wanted to build a similar garden enlisting NBRI's help. They discussed the merits of the case among themselves.

The concept had a great unique selling proposition (USP) for their country. There was a growing awareness about Ayurveda (which is thought to have originated around 5000 B.C.). Many such herbal gardens were springing up all around the country. PN's team wanted something that would distinguish their garden, something really unusual.

There was a brainstorm within the group. "Look, whichever park you go, you see signs forbidding people from touching leaves or flowers. Our garden will implore people to touch the flowers, beg them to pluck the leaves and eat them, because what they are eating is medicinal."

People agreed that anyone who visited this garden would agree that it was certainly unusual to see such signs. "We should also have walking tracks around the plants so that people can eat these medicines as part of their morning walks."

"How will they know what to eat and how much?"

"Well, needless to say, we'll need to create small placards about each plant."

The group could not wait any longer. They met PN and explained the idea. PN agreed to allocate a piece of the company campus garden to them.

The time went by swiftly for them. There were frustrations and moments of ecstasy. An acceptable landscape design was the subject of hot debate. Some wanted the landscaping on the basis of major ailments; some wanted the plants arranged according to the six

Indian seasons; and still others wanted the plants to be based on the needs of people in different zodiac signs.

Other employees appreciated the garden. Many actually took morning walks just to read about the plants and which ailments they cured. The achievement was a hot topic. The India herbal landscaping was a success.

PN called a meeting to discuss the Dutch client's request. But some members of the group were already in other projects, so only two members could join the Dutch project after a couple of weeks. The group was happy to take up the landscaping work as an additional responsibility, and those who were not in a position to travel pledged remote support.

PN was happy about this. But the group put forward a condition that the client's employees had to be involved in the garden. They said, "When the garden is ready, they will have the satisfaction of creating something of value for their own colleagues. We know the kind of happiness we experienced when we created our garden. We want them to feel the same about their garden."

The client agreed. They appreciated the viewpoint of PN's people and the opportunity being given to their employees.

The two members joined the client project after a few weeks. In the meantime, they had studied which plants would survive in the Netherlands. Their landscape design was ready.

The client's employees joined the gang. It was an enjoyable time for everyone involved. Soon a beautiful herbal landscape decorated the client's building.

The client was happy and gave encouraging testimonials to PN's people and to his company. The client used PN's pet word, *valufacture*, in their testimonials. They found great value in what the two young members of PN's company did for them, over and above the normal work of the project.

It was one of PN's happiest moments. His employees loved being part of the revolution, and they were greatly excited about the stamp they were putting on the map of a foreign city.

The media splashed rave stories about PN and his organization's contribution to society. They praised the employees' pride and sense of satisfaction. Management experts praised the various ways the employees could be engaged for better employee satisfaction.

PN felt a deep satisfaction that he had been able to provide a platform for his people to express themselves and be happy. It was yet another victory for John Galt!

Did his people stop after this achievement? Not at all. Encouraged by what they had achieved in the Netherlands, many more joined the group of herbal landscapers. They approached their own city guardians and asked to convert some gardens into herbal landscapes. The local bodies agreed if someone would maintain the gardens for free.

The city had unusual gardens where children could pluck the leaves and flowers. The team taught farmers in the neighboring villages how to grow medicinal herbs and how to set up nurseries. Many other clients wanted to replicate the Netherlands' experience. The list is endless.

A large number of employees of PN's company now had a forum to embark on the kind of journey that would previously only have been a dream!

ᘒᘒ

Reproduction Material

June 2, 2012: PN was looking at an invitation letter to be sent to M. F. Husain, the renowned painter. The invitation was for the inauguration of an art gallery owned by PN's employees.

The gallery had a large number of paintings, mainly reproductions of paintings by the great masters. What was unique was that PN's employees had created all the paintings. Each was accompanied by a write up explaining why the original was famous. It was a great collection and a great effort by his people to create an awareness of art appreciation.

PN's thought back to five years ago, when this new revolution had started in his organization. It was November 2006. PN had been invited to the Sloan School of Management at Massachusetts Institute of Technology for a conference entitled *The Emerging India*. After the conference, someone mentioned M. F. Husain's art exhibition at the Peabody Essex Museum. PN had not seen Husain before and did not want to miss this opportunity.

PN did not know much about art, but he was definitely fascinated by the artist. He was happy that he could actually meet the master himself, the great Husain, and spend some time with him.

Husain was curious to know what PN did for a living. PN told him about his organization and how it had become a matter of pride to the country, a feather in the cap of the emerging India.

Suddenly, Husain asked, "Could I visit your company?" PN could never say no to such requests.

Some weeks later, Husain visited PN's company at its fascinating campus. He saw the pride in everyone's eyes and was excited by what he saw. When he came back to PN's office after the visit, he told him, "PN, I want to create a painting for your company—*an emergent India*." It was one of PN's the happiest moments.

After some pleasantries, PN went down with Husain to see him off. As soon as he returned, he called a meeting with his team members. Once they gathered, PN told them the whole story and asked how they could use this event for the benefit of the organization.

Shoma, the PR person, spoke first. "PN, Husain is a well-known name. And it is great news that such a celebrity regards us as the representative of the new India. We can capitalize on this to create a good PR campaign."

"PN, a silly question." said Sam, head of Business Process Outsourcing. "Will he teach painting to some of our people?"

"This looks to be a good idea," said Suchitra, head of resourcing. "Some of our people would give their life to have Husain as their teacher."

Pawan, head of compensation and benefits, was excited at what Suchitra said. "I don't know if this will happen," he said, "but if it does, it will be a greatest incentive to people. But only top performers should be included in this."

There was a consensus that this was a very unusual reward and people would definitely love it. PN was aware that Sam was an amateur painter. So Sam was more than happy when PN asked him to manage the overall project.

He met Husain and got an amused Husain to agree to train about twenty people for a week. The grand day came when Husain's painting, *"The Emergent India"* was unveiled with great publicity. The painting was a depiction of the emerging spirit of India, an empowering canvas, a poetry that captured the country's new hope and confidence.

The names of the "trainees" to be taught by Husain were announced during the unveiling ceremony. The nominees were ecstatic about this new "reward."

It was an experience for Husain to teach painting to PN's people. Some of them knew little about painting. But at the end of the week, each of them had created a painting with a distinct Husain stamp of wild colors and heroic figures. The paintings were proudly displayed in a prominent place on the company premises.

This event created a new revolution within the company. Many people who were good at painting met Sam and coaxed him to start regular classes. They were ready to spend their weekends learning if the company would provide them with the space to work together. They were ready to pay tuition fees. And a new enterprise started with a lot of participation. Teachers from a local art school, Chitrakala Parishad, were happy to come and teach.

People came together on weekends, learned painting, learned about the great masters, and spent time together to share their happiness. They had never thought that it possible to complete their unfinished symphonies, their dreams of painting. For many, it was probably the best time of their lives.

During one such discussion, Sanjib, who loved to paint in an impressionist style, broached a topic. "Why don't we paint the famous paintings of the masters and display them in our offices?" Many were happy to do this. Someone said, "Sanjib, we are happy to do this, but who will understand your impressionist paintings?"

"Well, I can create a detailed write-up on each of the paintings," Sanjib said. "You all can create write-ups for your paintings. You can get help from many others in our organization."

People liked the idea. Many came forward to do the research and wrote up their findings about the paintings. The theme agreed for the paintings was the Impressionist painters. Each group was assigned a master whose painting they could reproduce.

They planned to create a hundred reproductions in twelve months.

One by one, the paintings started adorning the walls of the company premises. Below each painting, there was a small booklet describing the work, discussing its nuances and meaning. Each was highly educational. The artists were proud that their photographs and names appeared in those booklets, and superiors were proud too when they showed visitors what their employees had created.

The initiative became the talk of the town. People absolutely loved it. Many sent thank-you notes to PN, and others sent requests asking, "Why do you favor the painters? There are many of us who have other skills, and you must do something to fulfill our dreams too!"

PN was pleased with what was happening. Many people came up with ideas on initiatives in other arts or sciences. They were happy that their organization could start something around each one's unfinished dream.

PN visited the artists' hall on a weekend. He could see the many happy faces engrossed in recreating the masters' paintings. Each one of the paintings was a high quality job by the teachers and their students, PN thought. He was proud of his people.

Seeing PN walk around, many stopped their work and gathered around him. PN looked at his team with pride and said, "Great work, guys. I can clearly see the result of what you have created. Five hundred paintings are on display in an art gallery at the end of three years. Half of Bangalore's population has visited your gallery, which has become a must-visit destination for the tourists.

"Congratulations. Your contributions are of great value, both to the organization and to the city. You should be very proud of yourselves."

The dream he sold to his team three years earlier had actually became a reality.

His employees loved being part of this revolution. They raised funds internally to set up an art gallery and came up with an unusual name for it: *Reproduction*

Material, because all the paintings on display were going to be the reproductions of the world's greatest paintings. Some people objected to the name, but the artists went ahead with it. They wanted their venture to be bold, confident, and befitting the spirit of "the emergent India."

PN returned to the present. His eyes rested on the invitation letter on the table. The result of the hard work of his people was in front of him—an art gallery they owned with the paintings they created.

The great Husain inaugurated the gallery on September 17, 2012, his ninety-seventh birthday. The opening was a major milestone on a journey that had started when M. F. Husain visited PN's company and captured his people's pride on canvas.

What followed the inauguration was exciting. The media covered the opening and visitors soon flocked to see great masters' paintings. They brought guests to see and learn and enjoy.

It was one more victory for John Galt!

221B BAKER STREET
VERSUS MASTANI

April 28, 2010: PN was traveling to a place called Pabal to attend a unique event, the inauguration of a tourist center created by his employees.

What had been a small hamlet three years ago, was now going to be a great tourist destination, the place where Mastani, the goddess of beauty and romance, was buried on that same day 270 years ago.

Around three hundred employees had worked on the project for the past three years creating awareness, weaving stories around the romance of Mastani and Baji Rao and setting up a center for global tourists. Today, the world was going to see the fruits of their efforts.

PN took a trip down memory lane and recalled how it all started. It was September 12, 2006. PN was traveling to Pune. He had taken a day out from his schedule to visit a village called Pabal, where there was a technical school run by his schoolmate's parents.

The school was called Vigyan Ashram; it was an educational institution for technologies suitable to village economy. To be eligible for admission, a student had to be a school dropout.

PN had also heard that the school had a partnership with Massachusetts Institute of Technology in the United States and the Indian Institute of Technology for creating some technology breakthroughs for rural India. It was interesting, but far away from the city.

The school was on a small piece of land, yet holding a whole world of progressive technology. Young rural students in a remote drought-prone village managed it all. There were many success stories from supposedly unsuccessful students. PN thought it was just amazing!

After having lunch at the hostel mess, PN took a tour of the village. It was like any other village in India. But what caught PN's eye was the grave of Mastani.

Mastani, PN was told, was a dancer and singer and mistress of Baji Rao, prime minister of the Maratha Kingdom. Mastani, the villagers said, was a skilled horse-rider, skilled in spear throwing and swordsmanship. She accompanied Baji Rao on his military campaigns, inspiring him to extend the Maratha Empire in North India.

She was a renowned beauty. The local folklore said that she had such fair and translucent skin that when she swallowed the juice of her paan beeda (betel leaf with nuts and spices), the red color of the juice could be seen through the fair skin of her throat. It was a great, romantic story of the eighteenth century.

Her death too was equally fascinating. When Baji Rao died and was being cremated, Mastani walked into the flames of the pyre and ended her life alongside her lover.

Today, the grave of the beauty lay in a solitary and deserted place, which PN could not believe. PN could not believe that so few people knew about this story. He returned to his office promising himself to do something about it.

In a meeting with his management team, he told them about the Pabal school and asked how employees interested in public service could spend some time there to help students in their pursuit of technology.

Ganesh showed interest in the project. He was an MIT alumnus, so he could get access to MIT's work in Vigyan Ashram. He knew that many of his techno-savvy team members also wouldn't mind spending time there and contributing.

Then PN spoke about reviving the Mastani tomb. There was a general disapproval of this. Team members thought no one would visit such a place, and they felt there were better places for which they should provide sponsorship and seek publicity. Mastani's tomb was not worth the effort.

PN let the matter lie. Some time later, he had a chance to meet some of his UK employees, an enthusiastic group interested in tourism. They had recently completed a European tour and were inspired by the great tourist attractions they saw.

They were impressed by the skills of those countries that were creating tourist interests and the innovative ways they promoted tourism.

An example they gave was Sherlock Holmes' home, at 221B Baker Street in London. A tourist could visit the house, wear Holmes' bowler hat, smoke his famous pipe, have a photograph taken as a souvenir, buy replicas of Holmes' possessions, even read the same newspaper Holmes read. The tourist department had done a great job in creating this make-believe world.

"If other young people can take it as seriously as you have," PN said to the group, "we could do similar wonders." Then he told them the story of his visit to the Mastani grave. He explained that if they could get together and plan things, it would be possible to create a tourist center in Pabal. They knew PN well. Everything looked so simple to him. They also knew that they could trust PN to support them when they got stuck.

They put out feelers around the company and sought the support of a large number of people who were ready to be part of the project.

They had much to do. Some started doing research on Mastani's life. Others began working out what it takes to set up a tourist center, and others started working out the costs. Some went to stay in Pune and in Pabal. They spoke to the local government body, called the Panchayat, to the tourist department, and to the villagers to fill them with the enthusiasm to create a venture from which everyone would benefit.

Some enthusiasts planned to create videos to recreate the history; others planned for the sound and light programs. Some groups created a sustainability plan so that the center could go on functioning even after they had handed over control to the locals.

The work created lot of curiosity and interest in PN's company.

The plans were ready. Volunteers started coaching the villagers, creating local guides, helping them set up the essentials of a tourist center, including hygienic water, a clean environment, good food, clean toilets, and so on.

In the small village, all this built hope and enthusiasm to do something good. The news of what was happening in Pabal soon spread. Support for PN's volunteers came from many quarters.

And he came back to the present. PN's car neared the new tourist site. A huge crowd attended the launch. PN opened the tourist counter and handed over the key to the village head. The dream he had sold to his team three years ago had actually become a reality.

It was one more victory for John Galt!

∽

The VIBGYOR Ministry

December 23, 2008: PN was reading an internal report that contained a list of his people's accomplishments in totally new areas, not at all related to business.

His people were computer engineers, yet they dabbled in tissue culture. Many of them were teaching in colleges, some were teaching yoga to clients, some were teaching cookery to local women and creating a new life for them. Some were creating great paintings, and so on.

His people were investing their personal money, time, and effort in these activities. They were serving the community, and they were adding unique value to the business and adding hugely to the company brand value. Their passions and unmet dreams were being realized.

PN had succeeded in creating an Atlantis for them. And John Galt had secured some significant victories.

But all this was happening in an ad hoc manner. There was absolutely no guarantee how far this enthusiasm would sustain itself. The time had come to formalize it.

PN thought of asking his management members about this. When the team assembled, PN started with the customary words about where the organization was and where they were heading. Then he broached the topic he had in mind.

"Friends," PN said, "you are aware that we have been engaging our people in activities they are passionate about. We kicked off docendo discimus so that people could teach in colleges. We started the art initiative with the help of the great Husain, and people are now working on having their own art gallery. They learned cooking, then taught cooking and want to build their own theme restaurants. The herbal garden is getting ready for the visit of the Dutch queen. What do you think of the impact of our initiatives? How much fortune do you think we are reaping from the talent pool of people?"

Anand, the head of delivery strategy, was the first to speak. "PN, I remember I was the first person to say that we should stick to our business. And that all these activities should be outside the scope of our business strategy. But I have seen the benefits of this initiative over the past two years. People have become more enthusiastic, more productive, and more confident. They have become more well rounded. The customer satisfaction rating has improved. Our competitors are trying hard to figure out how we have managed to achieve all this.

"However, all this is happening in pockets. I do not know how much of this has become part of the 'system.' I think the time has come to build a strategy around it, to formalize it."

Dinesh, head of marketing, was gung ho about the initiative. In fact, he had coined a new term for the initiative: Corporate Social Responsibility for internal community, or iCSR. The idea sold well when his people talked about it as "employee engagement" during client presentations.

Mohan, the head of HR said, "I agree with Anand. Employee morale has increased a lot. There is a vast difference between the exit interviews of two years ago and those today. The top reason used to be 'development opportunity.' But it's no longer in the top three. Our employee engagement plan has been widely appreciated.

They feel our company is much more of a fun place now, though these activities are a really serious business."

Mohan continued, "I must also compliment Shoma and her team for the PR they did for all these activities.

Our brand recall on the college campuses and in the market has improved greatly. The initiative has aroused a lot of curiosity in candidates during interviews."

"But our recognition program is not very uniform for these people." said Pawan, head of compensation and benefits, "We do not have any defined guidelines for recognition in this area."

Jan, head of international business, who was from the Netherlands, said, "If such initiative were proposed in my country, I would never have believed that people would give their personal time for these activities. But from what I have seen over the past two years, I am sure I'll be able to rope in our international employees for similar activities in other countries."

AVL, QA head said, "I heard from some quarters that people are getting involved in all activities, irrespective of whether they have passions or not. So the results will not be as much as we want. We need to channel their efforts with some clear guidelines. Overall, this is a good initiative. We have added many best practices, which our Capability Maturity Model (CMM) assessors appreciated, during our recent assessment. Our scores in some of the People Capability Maturity Model (PCMM) processes, such as participatory culture, empowered workgroups, work environment, etc., have really taken a quantum leap. One of the comments from the assessors, though, could be taken into account when planning all this."

Suresh, the head of finance, was curious to know what the assessors' objection was.

"The comment wasn't to be taken as negative," AVL continued. "Their view was that if people's competencies are improving, why don't you create new ones in the areas in which those people are passionate and integrate them with your business competencies?"

"Fair point." PN said. "So you all agree that the time has come to formalize all this? If you feel there are business benefits, you must build this framework that you are talking about. I do not think I can add value to this. You are better equipped. Let's meet up next month. AVL, I think you should own the framework. Suresh, I am sure you will guide the team in funding."

The meeting disbanded. It was one more task for the business heads, but they did not mind. The press reports were really encouraging. Employee turnover was coming down. With a proper framework, they could reap better benefits.

AVL asked Gagan, the brainstorming expert, to co-ordinate the next meeting. The brainstorming session resulted in creation of various idea baskets, and actions were planned for each of them. Numerous ideas were floated.

"We must set quantifiable measures from this exercise."

"But how can we measure how much this activity contributed? There are so many intangibles involved, how are you going to measure the passions and the contribution?"

"You can't have one-to-one mapping of this initiative with employee satisfaction. There could be other hundred reasons why people are not happy."

"What about the new people? How are we going to get them involved? Will Sujoy (the training head) get involved in this? Will this be his official job responsibility?"

"Well, the training sessions conducted for awareness must be added to the per-employee training days. And Sujoy, therefore, must be involved."

"We must create a new competency framework as suggested by AVL. But who will define the scope and the competencies?"

"Well, we need to assign the overall responsibility to someone from the management team."

"But this becomes a full-time job."

"Then why don't we break these down into different groups?"

"How do we form groups? We don't even know what kind of activities are going to come in the future."

"We can group them into different sciences such as art, physics, chemistry, computer science, and so on."

"Ravi has some good suggestions. Let's hear him out."

"Some of you will be aware of something new happening in the schools," said Ravi, the operations head. "They are trying to implement what is called multiple intelligences. Howard Gardner, professor at the Harvard Graduate School of Education, created this concept. Gardner came up with eight categories of intelligences.

"We could create eight groups and assign them to eight of us. This will ensure that we have some scientific basis for the groups. Passions of people are nothing but what I call 'core intelligence.' These definitely map to Howard Gardner's groups of intelligences."

"Please, can you clarify, elaborate?"

"Oh, yes. Now take the example of Gagan's world environment group. Their area of interest is around nature and plants, the flora and the fauna. All the people engaged in these activities will come under the intelligence called the naturalist intelligence. Similarly, all the groups engaged in the dance competitions and part of the cricket and football teams will come under what Howard calls the kinesthetic intelligence. I see Pawan managing this group anyway. Being an avid sportsperson, he will be the natural choice, as we all know. We can allocate the remaining intelligences to other members in a similar manner."

There was not much discussion on who should own what because they knew each other's strong areas.

For example, linguistic intelligence went to Suchitra, who was good in languages and a good public speaker. Rachel enjoyed managing events, so the interpersonal intelligence group came under her. Ram always floored everyone with his sound logic, so logical intelligence went to him. Dhiraj owned rhythmic and musical intelligence because of his interest in music, and spatial intelligence was owned by, Sam, the painter. There was some debate on who should own intrapersonal intelligence, which is related to philosophy and spiritualism. Finally, most felt it should be owned by Jayant because of his networking skills and high emotional quotient.

The group felt the names of these intelligences would be difficult to remember in the day-to-day usage.

"Why don't we call them *houses*," Rachel suggested, "just as we used to call in our schools, such as Red House, Green House, etc.?"

Suchitra asked, "Ravi, don't we have some famous people attached to each of these intelligences?"

"Oh yes, we do," Ravi said. "For example, Dhiraj's music group could be the Mozart House, and Gagan's world environment group could be the Darwin House. Maybe I can find out more and let you all know about the famous people for the remaining intelligences?"

The first round of meeting ended. In the subsequent rounds, people deliberated on the priorities and objectives of each house, the processes and functions, the recognition parameters to measure the contributions made by individuals, the internal and external communication strategies, and so forth.

One important decision the group made was that each activity must be treated as a project and must follow the processes defined by the organization for projects. This helped accelerate the progress of formalizing the framework.

There was also some discussion on the topic of CSR.

Someone said, "We can reap a real benefit in the area of corporate social responsibility. We have thousands of hands now to work on this. What we do currently is little, considering the size of our organization."

"Good point. Let's attach CSR-related objectives to each house."

"Someone will have to help us convert the contribution in terms of money, though."

There was an agreement that each house and its projects must have quantifiable goals in the areas of:

- adding value to employees;

- adding value to clients;

- adding value to society; and

- adding value to the organization.

Then there was discussion on work-life balance. Someone said, "People are crying themselves hoarse that the current work level itself is an overload. They do not have any work-life balance. With this new initiative, they will have no personal time left."

"Let HR handle that. People have a limited view of what work-life balance is. When we give them a higher purpose in life, these issues will be taken care of automatically. Anyway, HR is the best body to take care of this."

"We must have some guidelines on the code of conduct so that people can behave accordingly."

"What about recognition for their contributions?"

"Each house can decide how they want to recognize and reward people. But keep the bar high."

"What about funding?"

"That should be decided on a case-by-case basis, but people need to understand that the organization will give support in providing space to conduct meetings, etc., or for their websites. But each house should self-fund its activities."

At the end of the discussions, everyone was excited about what they had created. They had lived up to their own expectations of being "thought leaders," and they could actually sense the excitement the iCSR framework was going to create in the industry and in the market. They saw new topics being debated among the management gurus.

The framework was presented to the group for comment. AVL summarized it:

- We want to call this initiative the "Talent++" initiative, a space where people's passions are realized;

- The overall vision is to provide a forum within which our employees can satisfy their passions so that we all, together, can contribute to our employees, our clients, and our society in a dramatically high measure;

- The areas of interest will be split in seven areas;

- Each group will be called a *house*;

- Each house will be represented by one color of the rainbow. The rainbow represents the dreams of people;

- Each house will be owned by one management member;

- Each house owner will have his or her own management committee elected from their group members;

- The allocation of houses is as below:

  - Shakespeare/ Violet/ Linguistic intelligence

  - Aristotle/ Indigo/ Logical intelligence

  - Van Gogh/ Blue/ Visual intelligence

  - Mozart/ Green/ Musical intelligence

  - Tiger Woods/ Yellow/ Kinesthetic intelligence

  - Darwin/ Orange/ Naturalistic intelligence

  - Oprah Winfrey Red/ Inter-personal intelligence

  - Confucius/ White/ Intra-personal intelligence

- Each house will have targets in the following areas:

  - value add to employees (internal client satisfaction)

  - clients (valufacture)

  - society (corporate social responsibility), and

- the organization (branding).

- The contribution from each house will be represented in monetary terms. (We are still working on how to quantify the intangibles);

- Each activity will be run and reported as a project and will follow our standard process areas for managing projects;

- These projects will produce reports and metrics similar to the regular projects;

- They will also create project briefs at the end of the project for our KM (knowledge management) repository;

- Our official global resourcing tool will be used to secure people for each project;

- Each employee's competencies and passions will be noted in the competency database so that the project managers can select properly;

- The communications group will use the information from the monthly project reports and the project closure reports and briefs for:

  - internal communication and awareness,

  - external communication and branding,

- communication for internet,

- text for the annual report, and

- material for market collateral.

- There will be annual individual and team awards in each house. Each house will publish criteria for the awards;

- There will be guidelines for seniority ranking in each house, similar to the one we have in the military;

- The seniority ranking will be captured in the employee database and will be reflected in terms of stars on the employee ID cards. This will ensure that the bar for people to earn stripes is set high;

- The contribution from each employee will be measured and used for assigning the seniority and stars in terms of:

  - the number of hours of training,

  - the number and reader ratings of write-ups and awareness pieces created,

  - the person-days spent on the Talent++ projects,

- the number of papers and publications submitted to national and international forums, and

- the number of testimonials from the clients.

- Some projects could be run jointly by more than one house. E.g., adopting a village—the Shakespeare house will send linguists to write about what is happening, the van Goghs to teach painting, the Oprahs to manage the village events, the Darwins to teach them hygiene and maybe organic farming techniques, and so forth;

- Each house will have a website to host the following:

  - a vision statement for the house,

  - guidelines for the new joiners and a code of conduct,

  - eligibility criteria for joining and a skills requirement,

  - an events calendar,

  - objectives, budgets, and spending for the year,

  - status of each running project,

  - research papers,

- success stories and testimonials,

- a list of groups and members,

- parameters for earning stripes, ribbons, and medals,

- press coverage,

- entities of repute with which to partner,

- and the names of global awards for which to strive.

- Awareness about Talent++ will be an integral part of the new joiners' induction program;

- As far as possible, the projects will be in partnership with known gurus in the area, and each house will maintain a list of the approved partners;

- Each house will maintain a list of national and international awards to participate in so members can conduct their work in line with the parameters set for these;

- We need to copyright some of our concepts.

PN looked at his team with pride and concluded, "Great work, as usual, guys. I can clearly see the results of what you defined today. At least ten percent of our employees engaged in the activities that they are passionate about. Our attrition rate has been reduced by one percent. Brand value improved by 0.5 percent year on year, and an annual CSR contribution is 0.2 percent of our revenue.

"Congratulations. You have done a great service to the organization, to our people, to the community, and to our customers."

The dream he sold to his lieutenants actually became a reality. His employees loved being part of the revolution. The media splashed rave stories about PN's organization's contribution to the society. The management gurus loved the new buzzwords and started building case studies around those.

This was a great victory for John Galt!

Dear Readers, now the ball is in your court. Use PN's experiments in your organization; bring happiness to your people; add value to society; give benefits of your valufacture to your customers; generate fortune from the untapped talent pool of your organization.

Is This Some 'Management' Book?

Is this a book written only as a management tool? What is in it for an individual?

I would like to share some of my real-life experiences. They will convey how important it is for all us to find out what our core is and how it benefits us, not only individually but also the people around us.

One of my friends was assigned an assistant who had been rejected by other departments. My friend found something special in this person. He had a flair for numbers, but if you asked him to write reports, he would mess up. He also had great talent for music. My friend encouraged this talent and also changed his work pattern, allocating him all the number-crunching jobs of the department. Soon a happy man emerged out of this under-achieving person. It was a fortunate event for him to have such a boss who came to his aid and brought out his talents.

Another incident I remember occurred when we wanted to give our boss a special gift. He was leaving the organization. We decided that we would jointly create a painting for him. But none of us knew how to paint in oil. We went on a hunt to find someone in our organization who could guide us. We found one in Sanjib, who did a fantastic job of helping us work on the painting. I have no words to explain the appreciation our boss showed when he received our creation. In the process of creating the painting, our "teacher" became a celebrity for this talent, but it was not the one for which he was hired by the organization.

Each one of us has talents, but we hardly have time to discover them or use them.

I once attended a workshop conducted by the founding members of a school in Indianapolis called Key Learning Community. It is a multiple-intelligences school based on Howard Gardner's theory. It was amazing how they groomed the students. The greatest moment was when they showed a series of one-minute video clips of a young boy from four years old until he completed his schooling. Each clip was a presentation from the boy on a topic he loved the most at that point in time. We could see the transformation of a shy young boy into a confident young man who, by the time he grew up, knew what his calling was. It is a great lesson to young parents about how they could allocate small projects to their children and capture their journey on videos. You would give the greatest present to the child when you present the videos to him or her.

I remember seeing long time ago a painting by Pablo Picasso. It was from one of his famous Minotaur series. The painting showed the Minotaur pulling a heavy cart, carrying his pregnant wife, who was heavy with a child. The Minotaur looks burdened with responsibilities and is trying hard to meet his obligations of taking care of his family.

What caught my attention was the small rainbow in the corner of the cart he was pulling—a rainbow of his dream. He knew this rainbow kept him alive. He hoped he would one day pull it out, dust it off, and engage in the pursuit of realizing his dream. Until then, he had to keep pulling his heavy cart. Don't you think this painting represents each of us?

My advice is not to wait for some free time to be available to you to realize such happiness. You will never get it. Take a breather, find out your passions and talents, find out who else has similar passions, and collaborate to live your dream, even if for a short while during the day, during a week or a month.

We live in the Internet era and can easily find friends from any part of the world. The world has become a small place, and people with talents similar to yours can be reached wherever they are on this globe. Start your journey, collaborate, and be happy.

ACKNOWLEDGEMENTS

I am aware that some of you will be excited to start similar initiatives in your organization after reading this book. At the same time, others will outright trash this idea as a waste of energy and money because it may not bring about the utopian benefits I have written about.

You may say, "Well, you have already called the book a fairytale. I assume all this is not possible in real life."

I want to share with you some interesting feedback I received from many of my colleagues and friends when I sent them the manuscript and asked for their response.

One of the CEOs responded: "This may be relevant to your IT industry, but not for my company. Most of my people are blue-collar workers, and if I asked them "What is your passion? I want you to realize your dreams.", they would think I had lost my beans. Some of them would actually think, I have some secret agenda to make more money for myself!"

Others expressed reservations about the real-world implementation of these ideas. At the same time, I have some beautiful moments to share.

The first was when my boss, Sushil, asked me to extend my vacation so that I could complete this book. He knew how important it was to me, and he wanted me to experience the ecstasy of doing something that was so dear to me. He also publicized the fact that I was going to come back only after the book was complete. This forced me to work day and night and complete the book (though, of course, I loved this toil!).

Then there was a very encouraging note from one of our senior management members, Jan Willem van Doorn, who felt the idea was good enough to be implemented. He also shared with me some examples. One of them concerned how the Dutch managers came together to paint something around the company values and how all those paintings still hang in our office in Amstelveen, Netherlands.

Quite a few of my colleagues came up with useful comments that helped me shape the book into its current form; Rachna Patel, Ravinder Mandayam, Visvanathan, Gaurishankar, Sarvottam Kini, Justin Hooper, Shrinidhi Sharma, Deepak Shenoy, Ashit Choudhury, and Nagesh Rao to name a few.

One of my colleagues from the UK, Gillian Hardy, was the first one I looked to for correcting my English. She kept her promise in doing a ruthless review.

The greatest support came from my family.

I remember when I read my manuscript to my wife, Sheila. She said nothing; she just shed a few tears. When she calmed down, I asked her the reason for her response. "I was just imagining the blissful work-life the people will have in such companies that will implement this," she said. "Sometimes, when I think of a company, it looks to me like a giant sugarcane crusher. The employee, when he gets in, is full of sweet juice; what comes out at the end of the career is bagasse, the dry residue."

I would pester my son Satej all the while to help me build the book. I would wake him up in the middle of the night to tell him about it. He showed a lot of patience with me.

My eighty-year-old mother, Aparna, my two sisters, Shyamal and Padma and brother, Nitin were full of praise for the book and did some reviewing; so were my cousins, Srikar and Sandeep, who gave me some contacts so that I could meet people to discuss details about their companies.

My brother-in-law Prasad sold the idea to the CEO of the company he works for, of promoting a heritage center that is located near their production unit.

I have no doubt that the thinking behind this book will catch the imagination of many who are in the thick of talent management in their companies, and we will see less and less of bagasse in times to come!

It was by coincidence that I was introduced to Linda Roberts, who is a proofreader, among other things. She went through the manuscript with a fine-tooth comb to check for language acceptability and declared the book worth reading by good people who want to make the world beautiful. I am grateful for the confidence she gave me.

I am grateful to my CEO, Abhay Gupte, who agreed to write the foreword.

FOR FURTHER READING

The various books I read in the course of my life's journey have provided great joy and inspiration. I am grateful to these authors and wish to pay my respect by writing a few lines about some of them and their books.

Ayn Rand

I must have read Ayn Rand's books *Fountainhead* and *Atlas Shrugged* about thirty years ago. Their plots are still fresh in my mind. Rand's books are about excellence in human beings. Her heroes and heroines are the perfect human beings. The characters of Howard Roark (*Fountainhead*) and John Galt (*Atlas Shrugged*) encourage you to look inward to find your potential and release it for your own sake.

Atlas Shrugged was first published in 1957. Its theme is what happens to the world when the prime movers go on strike. The book is a picture of the world with its motor cut off.

The book starts with a question "Who is John Galt?".

The reader is curious to know and learns later that he is the person who is meeting the genius of the world to convince them to come and stay in his secret city Atlantis.

What I learned from the book was the importance one should attach to understanding one's potential, to living as a whole human being.

After every section of my book, you will find a mention about John Galt. It is my salute to him.

Howard Gardner

Howard Gardner's work on multiple intelligences opened a new area of understanding to me. Many of us have never looked within to learn what our intelligences are. But once you are aware, you can plan how to grow and make a real difference to yourself and those around you.

The education world is changing for better in the recent times because many schools have embraced Gardner's work and are implementing it with a mission of bringing out the real potential of their students.

Gardner's book *Multiple Intelligences – New Horizons* provides a good insight on how to nurture intelligence from early childhood.

Ken Blanchard

I have been a fan of Ken Blanchard for twenty-five years. Blanchard invented the genre of business fables. His books are short stories that carry powerful messages and tools to bring about excellence in organizations and in individuals. I was so impacted by his style that I wrote my book in the same genre.

The first book I read of Blanchard's was *The One Minute Manager*, written with Spencer Johnson. It haunted me for a long time. This small book traces the journey of a young manager and gives the reader a mantra on how to become a great manager by using three small one-minute actions: one-minute goal setting, one-minute praising, and one-minute reprimand. Each of Blanchard's books provides tips on how to excel.

Edward de Bono

I have been reading Edward de Bono's books for about twenty-five years. He has contributed immensely in the area of innovation and creativity. He coined the now popular term *lateral thinking*. I had the fortune of learning a few lateral thinking techniques from his brother, Peter de Bono. De Bono's reading always helped me think creatively throughout my career.

I picked the word *valufacture* for my book from his book titled *Sur/Petition: Going Beyond Competition*. This book provides great insight and a number of examples of how to beat competition using surpetition techniques.

Marcus Buckingham

His books *Now, Discover Your Strength*, written with Donald O. Clifton, and *First, Break All the Rules*, written with Curt Coffman, are a great help in understanding how good managers develop talents and grow people. Research by Gallup over the past seventy years is distilled in these books and provides great implementation techniques.

Tom Peters

I read *In Search of Excellence* by Tom Peters and Robert Waterman some twenty years ago. The book is a study of various organizations and what they did to excel and become the best in their class. The authors found eight common themes that they argued were responsible for the success of the top forty-three Fortune 500 companies. The book is full of anecdotes and examples to make it a great read.

A. P. J. Abdul Kalam and Nandan Nilekani

A. P. J. Abdul Kalam, former president of India and also known as the "Missile Man of India," and Y. S. Rajan wrote a treatise called *2020—A Vision for the New Millennium*. The book is a study of India's core strengths and how they can be leveraged to develop the economy. The book gives a clear vision for the future till the year 2020.

Nandan Nilekani, co-founder and ex-CEO of one of India's renowned IT companies, Infosys, wrote a book titled *Imagining India, Ideas for the New Century*.

Both Adbul Kalam and Nandan Nilekani create a bright, energetic vision for India. Both talk about the need for mass education, better infrastructure, better public health, and leveraging from technology.

My firm belief is that the private corporate world holds the key to bringing these visions to reality. It has the entrepreneurial capability, it has creativity, it has a huge mass of employees waiting for their intellectual pool to be exploited for the public good and the good of the world. The dreams of these visionaries can be easily achieved when the will (public) and the power (private) make it a joint agenda.

Stephen R. Covey

A suggested reading list in the area of personality development would not be complete without Stephen R. Covey. More than twenty million copies of his books have been sold. His most famous book *The 7 Habits of Highly Effective People* is said to be the most influential business book of twentieth century. It provides useful tips on how to live your life's journey.

ABOUT THE AUTHOR

Prabodh Sirur has worked in the Information Technology and Financial Services industries for over thirty-five years. He is currently Staff Operations Manager in India for Logica, a leading IT and business services company that employs 39,000 people across thirty-six countries.

In his current position, as well as in his previous managerial roles, the primary responsibility has been as a motivator of employees. He works with employees to resolve various problems related to performance improvement, career progression, and conflict resolution.

"This has given me a perspective," Sirur says, "about what a person's needs are, how a person can be motivated, and what the best possible course is for employee engagement."

He has come to believe that the corporate world has the power to make the world more beautiful, sometimes by partnering with governments and sometimes by picking up the threads that the governments leave off.

Sirur has a Masters in Management Accounting. Today he lives in Bangalore, India, with his wife, Sheila. Their son, Satej, resides in New York.